MW01050113

# THE

# HOPEFUL

# DISCIPLE

+ + +

*A Bible Study Based on the New Testament Letters of First and Second Peter*
*by*
*Robert L. Tasler*

# NOTICE OF RIGHTS

# AUTHOR'S NOTE

The Bible references used in this work are from the English Standard Version, 2011 edition, an updating of the Revised Standard Version of 1971, published by Crossway Bibles. In this study the New Testament text is printed in italics and the Old Testament passages are also in bold type. I thank my loving and loyal wife Carol for her valuable counsel and proof-reading of the content of this Bible Study.

# ALSO BY THE AUTHOR
(Paperback and E-Book)

**Daily Walk With Jesus**
**Daily Word From Jesus**
**Spreading The Word**
**Reflections**
**Murder At Palm Park**
**Matrimony At Palm Park**
**Miracle at Palm Park**
**Bobby Was A Farmer Boy**

(E-Book only)

**Country Preacher**
**Small Town Preacher**
**Immigrant Son**

(Bible Study)
**The Hopeful Disciple**

# Table of Contents

# Preface to First and Second Peter

Peter is a good person to study if you want to get a glimpse into the life of one of God's ordinary yet remarkable disciples. He was probably older than most of the others, and certainly more outspoken, having a tendency to talk first and think later. He was a leader of the disciples and correctly believed Jesus had a special place for him in His small band of followers.

Peter's letters were written in a style of Greek that was not as refined as Paul's or John's since he did not have their education. Peter was a laborer, a fisherman whose hands were used to handling nets, not pen and ink. He was used to thinking on the fly, not writing and reshaping his thoughts.

Peter's two letters were extremely valuable to the early church, and he may have written more. But the two we have are wonderful examples of the godly ruminations of a man who had sat at the feet of the Master and was able to share his reflections with others.

Peter explains important teachings in his two letters. He urges people to have a living hope in Jesus, those who were "living stones" in God's spiritual house and will suffer for following their Lord. They had been called by God who knew beforehand that they would believe in Him. They therefore must avoid false prophets and respect the true shepherds of God.

He tells of Christ's descent into hell and His impending return, so they should be ready. These are just a few of the important concepts Peter imparts to all who have read the words of his two letters to Christians dispersed throughout the Roman empire and the world.

Peter urged them to love one another, to trust God and obey the emperor and his laws. He did not proclaim a new social order, but to follow the one they had with love and justice. He related these important concepts, knowing his hearers would be empowered to follow them because of Jesus. Peter often quotes the Old Testament, always in light of the New Covenant made when Jesus was put to death but raised again to show He was truly God's Son.

Peter is one of us, as were all the apostles. He made his mistakes, some boldly and some sadly, but he was reconciled to Christ and God's people. His messages in First and Second Peter are more precious than earthly treasurers to people of the ages, for they are words of life. God bless you as you hear them once again, perhaps for the first time.

While I encourage use of several Bible versions, I have used the English Standard Version in these sessions for the purpose of studying the same words. God bless all who read <u>The Hopeful Disciple.</u> This book can also, of course, be used for individual Bible study.

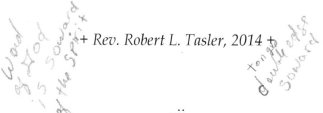

+ *Rev. Robert L. Tasler, 2014* +

vii

# Dedication

*To Pastor Darrell and Wanda Howanitz, tireless and faithful co-workers in the Kingdom and good friends over the years.*

*To my winter friends at Trinity Lutheran Church, Casa Grande, Arizona, for their friendship and faithfulness in studying the scriptures during our years together.*

# "The Hopeful Disciple"

*A Study of the Letters of St. Peter*

## Session #1

+ + +

### Overview of 1 Peter

**AUTHOR**

I Peter 1:1 states the author is Peter. The contents, character of the letter, the historical references and style of writing support this. Its themes and concepts reflects Peter's experiences and associations during the time of Jesus' ministry and his subsequent ministry. References show he is familiar with Paul and some of his letters. Thus, his expression of some of Paul's themes is not surprising.

While most scholars agree that Peter wrote these two epistles, some claim that the style of Greek in this letter is beyond Peter's competence. Some also say Peter could not speak Greek at all, and therefore could not be the author. But Peter surely did speak and write in Greek, as did the other apostles.

1. How would you determine who was the author of a letter?
   Context, Return address

2. Why is it important to know who is the author of a Bible book?
   Someone of Apostlic Stature

2 Peter 3:1 refers to a previous letter Peter had written. Writings of two church fathers, Clement of Rome and Polycarp of Smyrna, one of John's

1

disciples who served the Church after Peter's death, show a familiarity with 1 Peter. They and other early church fathers did not doubt Peter was the author.

## DATE

It is probable this letter was written in the early AD 60's, just prior to Peter's death. It can't be placed earlier than 60 since it shows familiarity with Paul's prison letters, Colossians and Ephesians, which are dated no earlier than 60. It can't be placed later than 67-68 AD, the probable time Peter was martyred during Nero's reign.

3. How would knowing the date of a letter help in understanding its message? References to the time & places to understand

## RECIPIENTS

1 Peter is written to the Christians of the five provinces of Asia Minor (Pontus, Galatia, Cappadocia, Asia, and Bithynia). They are exiles, either having been forced away from Israel by their newfound faith, or those who already lived away from Israel and had become Christians through the witness of others.

Acts 2:8-11 says on the first Pentecost the people heard the disciples preaching of Jesus in many languages, including that of people from *"Mesopotamia, Judea and Cappadocia, Pontus and Asia, Phrygia and Pamphylia."* Peter's first letter could have been read by some of the people who were actually there on that miraculous day and took their newfound faith in Jesus of Nazareth home with them to share.

4. How could knowing the recipients affect your understanding of a letter?

5. How important are written letters in our culture today?

## PLACE

1 Peter 5:13 indicates Peter was in "Babylon" when he wrote his first letter. Since he was most certainly not in ancient Babylon, he was either in (1) Egyptian Babylon, a military outpost or, (2) Rome or even (3) Jerusalem, since "Babylon" is most probably used symbolically. Tradition and certain early writers have indicated 1 Peter was written in Rome.

6. What kind of problems does one encounter when reading a letter written to someone other than yourself?

7. Some say reading a Bible letter is like hearing only half of a conversation between two people. How is that a good comparison?

## THEMES

Different readers have found 1 Peter to have different major themes. It has been characterized as a letter of hope, of separation, of suffering-persecution-glory, of pilgrimage, of courage, and of the true grace of God. 1 Peter 5:12 states Peter has written *"encouraging you and testifying that this*

3

*is the true grace of God."* That verse could be a definitive description of the letter, but the letter incorporates numerous other themes. 1 Peter 1:13 - 5:11 is a continual series of exhortations. Some have felt 1 Peter was to be delivered to those just baptized into the Christian faith, and 2 Peter was a message to the entire congregation.

8. Why is it important to understand the theme of any letter, but especially a letter of Holy Scripture?


9. How can knowing this letter is the Word of God give us hope?


*Thank You, Lord, that You have given us Your Holy Word through the apostles and prophets. Help us trust it and live according to it. Amen*

NOTES:

# "The Hopeful Disciple"

*A Study of the Letters of St. Peter*

## *Session #2*
## The First Letter of Peter 1:1-12

**+ + +**

**1** *¹ Peter, an apostle of Jesus Christ, to those who are elect exiles of the Dispersion in Pontus, Galatia, Cappadocia, Asia, and Bithynia, ² according to the foreknowledge of God the Father, in the sanctification of the Spirit, for obedience to Jesus Christ and for sprinkling with his blood: May grace and peace be multiplied to you. ³ Blessed be the God and Father of our Lord Jesus Christ! According to his great mercy, he has caused us to be born again to a living hope through the resurrection of Jesus Christ from the dead, ⁴ to an inheritance that is imperishable, undefiled, and unfading, kept in heaven for you, ⁵ who by God's power are being guarded through faith for a salvation ready to be revealed in the last time. ⁶ In this you rejoice, though now for a little while, if necessary, you have been grieved by various trials, ⁷ so that the tested genuineness of your faith — more precious than gold that perishes though it is tested by fire — may be found to result in praise and glory and honor at the revelation of Jesus Christ. ⁸ Though you have not seen him, you love him. Though you do not now see him, you believe in him and rejoice with joy that is inexpressible and filled with glory, ⁹ obtaining the outcome of your faith, the salvation of your souls. ¹⁰ Concerning this salvation, the prophets who prophesied about the grace that was to be yours searched and inquired carefully,*

5

*[11] inquiring what person or time the Spirit of Christ in them was indicating when he predicted the sufferings of Christ and the subsequent glories. [12] It was revealed to them that they were serving not themselves but you, in the things that have now been announced to you through those who preached the good news to you by the Holy Spirit sent from heaven, things into which angels long to look.*

+  +  +

Religion in the first century world was closely tied to the social and political life of the times. To follow another religion than that of the current culture could be construed as disloyal, especially when "emperor worship" was the official religion. Being a Christian was like wishing bad crops on the farmers or social unrest on the society. Being a Christian meant being different from the culture in every sense of the word.

1. What is the difference between a disciple and an apostle?


2. Why did Peter refer to the people as *"exiles?"*


3. What does *"foreknowledge"* mean in verse 2? *"Sanctification?"*
   God chosen

4. What do you think *"sprinkling with his blood"* means?
   Confess Accept Him as our lord & saviour
   Baptism, communion

5. How can these terms help give us hope?

6

6. Are Christians today called upon to be "different" from their culture?


7. What is the basis for Peter's joy in verses 3-5?


8. What *"inheritance"* is being kept for them?


9. What are verses 6-7 speaking of?


10. (Complete) Trials "test" our __Faith__. They make it _____and _____because it is tested by _____.


11. How do verses 8-9 define faith?


12. (Complete) Verses 10-11 refer to Old Testament _____ who predicted the _____ would come, and also predicted His _____ and His _____.


13. How does verse 12 tell us who the Old Testament prophets were serving?


14. Who would you say is meant by, *"those who preached the good news to you"* in verse 12?

7

15. What do you think is meant by the phrase *"things into which angels long to look"?*


16. The title of this Bible Study is <u>The Hopeful Disciple.</u> Look at verses 3-6 and summarize what Peter's basis for hope is.


17. In light of this, how would you define "hope" as we use it in our every day conversation?


*Thank You, Lord Jesus, for the hope You give us by Your life, death and resurrection, that we might be forgiven and acceptable to the Father. Amen*

NOTES:

# "The Hopeful Disciple"
### *A Study of the Letters of St. Peter*

## *Session #3*
## The First Letter of Peter 1:13-25
### + + +

**1** [13] *Therefore, preparing your minds for action, and being sober-minded, set your hope fully on the grace that will be brought to you at the revelation of Jesus Christ.* [14] *As obedient children, do not be conformed to the passions of your former ignorance,* [15] *but as he who called you is holy, you also be holy in all your conduct,* [16] *since it is written,* **"You shall be holy, for I am holy."** [17] *And if you call on him as Father who judges impartially according to each one's deeds, conduct yourselves with fear throughout the time of your exile,* [18] *knowing that you were ransomed from the futile ways inherited from your forefathers, not with perishable things such as silver or gold,* [19] *but with the precious blood of Christ, like that of a lamb without blemish or spot.* [20] *He was foreknown before the foundation of the world but was made manifest in the last times for the sake of you* [21] *who through him are believers in God, who raised him from the dead and gave him glory, so that your faith and hope are in God.* [22] *Having purified your souls by your obedience to the truth for a sincere brotherly love, love one another earnestly from a pure heart,* [23] *since you have been born again, not of perishable seed but of imperishable, through the living and abiding word of God;* [24] *for* **"All flesh is like grass and all its glory like the flower of grass. The grass withers, and the flower falls,** [25] *but the word* *of the Lord remains forever."* And this is the word that was preached to you.

+ + +

In this section, Peter applies the Good News of Jesus Christ to the lives of the people. Two words are important here, obedience and love. The behavior of a Christian is always based on the grace of God, not on self-righteousness acts. God gives both the motive and the power for our godly behavior.

Disciplined behavior avoids extremes of conduct. Christians are to be conformed to the character of Jesus. The death and resurrection of Jesus make it possible for us to enjoy our new and free relationship with God, because He is both the author and finisher of our redemption.

When we trust the Gospel of Jesus Christ, we will have God's power to live a new and hopeful life. Everything else may fall and fail in life, but the Gospel of Jesus Christ remains forever.

1. For what does Peter want the people to prepare? Why?

2. To what do you think *"passions of your former ignorance"* might refer? What similar passions of ignorance are being passed around among people today?

3. Where is the Old Testament passage quoted in verse 16?

4. In verse 17, on what basis does God judge us?

5. How then should we live as Christians?

6. What are the *"futile ways inherited from your forefathers"?*

7. What *"futile ways"* do we see around us today?

8. How were we ransomed from them (verse 18)?

9. Who was *"foreknown"* but now is *"made manifest"?*

10. How does verse 21 say people are made believers?

11. Who *"purified your souls"?*

12. What is the result of that purification, according to verse 22?

13. What do you think is meant by being *"born of imperishable seed"* in verse 23?


14. What Old Testament verse is quoted in verse 24?


15. Why do you think Peter quotes this verse here?


16. How do the words *"but the word of the Lord remains forever"* give us hope?


17. When or how was *"this word"* (verse 25) preached to them?


*Thank You, Lord Jesus, for being our Savior. Help us live lives that give honor to Your name. Amen*

NOTES:

# "The Hopeful Disciple"

*A Study of the Letters of St. Peter*

## Session #4
## The First Letter of Peter 2:1-12

+ + +

2 *¹ So put away all malice and all deceit and hypocrisy and envy and all slander. ² Like newborn infants, long for the pure spiritual milk, that by it you may grow up into salvation —  ³ if indeed you have tasted that the Lord is good. ⁴ As you come to him, a living stone rejected by men but in the sight of God chosen and precious, ⁵ you yourselves like living stones are being built up as a spiritual house, to be a holy priesthood, to offer spiritual sacrifices acceptable to God through Jesus Christ. ⁶ For it stands in Scripture:* **"Behold, I am laying in Zion a stone, a cornerstone chosen and precious, and whoever believes in him will not be put to shame."** *⁷ So the honor is for you who believe, but for those who do not believe,* **"The stone that the builders rejected has become the cornerstone,"** *⁸ and* **"A stone of stumbling and a rock of offense."** *They stumble because they disobey the word, as they were destined to do. ⁹ But you are a chosen race, a royal priesthood, a holy nation, a people for his own possession, that you may proclaim the excellences of him who called you out of darkness into his marvelous light. ¹⁰ Once you were not a people, but now you are God's people; once you had not received mercy, but now you have received mercy. ¹¹ Beloved, I urge you as sojourners and exiles to abstain from the passions of the flesh, which wage war against your soul. ¹² Keep your*

*conduct among the Gentiles honorable, so that when they speak against you as evildoers, they may see your good deeds and glorify God on the day of visitation.*

+ + +

Peter is urging the early Christians to live differently from those around them. While being restricted by many laws, people under Roman rule tended to follow their basic urges more than display moral values. It was daily life to be malicious or deceitful. Hypocrisy, slander and envy were a normal part of their daily lives if they wished to have freedom of speech and thought. This was also somewhat true in the Jewish church.

Peter continues his exhortations to live the way God would have them live. They are His beloved people, the recipients of His grace. They are a royal, chosen and holy people of God, so they must abstain from the ways of the world and conduct themselves so that others will want to know this Jesus whom they worship. Peter encourages them to share the Gospel with people by their loving and kind actions which were quite unknown in the worldliness of Roman culture.

1. How could being like newborn babes in their faith (verse 2) help them?

2. (Complete) In verses 4-5, Peter calls Jesus a _____ stone rejected by people but chosen by God. Christians are living _____ being built up as a spiritual _____ and a holy _____.

14

3. Where is the Old Testament prophesy found in verse 6?




4. What is the *"honor"* for believers in verse 7?




5. Who is Jesus to those who do not believe?




6. Why do they stumble?




7. What *"destined"* unbelievers to stumble (verse 7)?




8. (Complete): *You are a_____ race, a royal _____, a_____ nation, a people for his own _____, that you may proclaim the _____ of him who called you out of _____ into his marvelous _____.*

9. Verse 9 should give us tremendous hope. We are not just a struggling people, but God's holy people, a royal priesthood of His own making. Why is that so amazing?



10. Why are Christians *"God's people"* according to verse 10?



11. Because of this, what does Peter urge the people to do?

12. What is *"sanctification"* (verse 2)? How does it help in what Peter is urging them to do?

13. What is a *"sojourner"* mentioned in verse 11? How would this affect how they lived?

14. Why does verse 11 tell us it is needful to keep one's life pure?

15. How are the last words of verse 14 similar to what Jesus said in Matthew 5:16?

*Father God, thank You for choosing us to be Your people. Help us to give honor to Your name, that others may also give You glory, now and eternally. Amen*

NOTES:

# "The Hopeful Disciple"

*A Study of the Letters of St. Peter*

## *Session #5*
## The First Letter of Peter 2:13-25

✝ ✝ ✝

**2** *¹³ Be subject for the Lord's sake to every human institution, whether it be to the emperor as supreme, ¹⁴ or to governors as sent by him to punish those who do evil and to praise those who do good. ¹⁵ For this is the will of God, that by doing good you should put to silence the ignorance of foolish people. ¹⁶ Live as people who are free, not using your freedom as a cover-up for evil, but living as servants of God. ¹⁷ Honor everyone. Love the brotherhood. Fear God. Honor the emperor. ¹⁸ Servants, be subject to your masters with all respect, not only to the good and gentle but also to the unjust. ¹⁹ For this is a gracious thing, when, mindful of God, one endures sorrows while suffering unjustly. ²⁰ For what credit is it if, when you sin and are beaten for it, you endure? But if when you do good and suffer for it you endure, this is a gracious thing in the sight of God. ²¹ For to this you have been called, because Christ also suffered for you, leaving you an example, so that you might follow in his steps. ²² He committed no sin, neither was deceit found in his mouth. ²³ When he was reviled, he did not revile in return; when he suffered, he did not threaten, but continued entrusting himself to him who judges justly. ²⁴ He himself bore our sins in his body on the tree, that we might die to sin and live to righteousness. By his wounds you have been healed.*

*²⁵ For you were straying like sheep, but have now returned to the Shepherd and Overseer of your souls.*

+  +  +

Chapters two through four contain some of the most important passages in the New Testament. Peter has assured the believers they have been born anew by the power of Christ and His Word. They will taste the goodness of God in all He does for them.

They are now part of the elect people of God. What will their new status mean? They are living stones and are being built into a temple far superior to the Jewish Temple (which will be destroyed a few years after Peter's writing). They are part of the New Israel, of which Christ is the Cornerstone. The Church is now the holy community of God and each believer is a priest within the community of believers.

All the great words and phrases used to describe the Old Testament Chosen People can now be applied to the Christian Church. The Church now inherits all the promises of God. By proclaiming and living Christ's Word they declare the wonderful deeds of God in Jesus Christ.

1. If we believers now have such a privileged status, why must we also submit ourselves to human institutions (verse 13-14)?

honor.
Gods will

2. How might believers today, *"silence the ignorance of foolish people"* (verse 15)? Which foolish people?

3. What does *"Live as free people"* mean? (Verse 16) How might some believers use their freedom as a *"cover-up"* for evil?

4. How can Christians today honor their leaders when they don't agree with them?

5. How can verse 18 apply to today's employees and employers? What if the boss is unfair or heavy-handed?

6. In verse 18-20, Peter speaks about suffering unjustly. How can it be that *"it is a gracious thing in the sight of God"* if we suffer unjustly?

7. How can our suffering ever benefit us? What about Jesus' suffering?

8. In verse 21, Peter compares Christ's suffering with our own. He is our example. What does this mean for Christians suffering around the world today?

9. Verses 22-23 almost sound like Isaiah's "Suffering Servant." Read Isaiah 53:3-6 for a comparison.

10. Where in the Gospel of John does Jesus speak of sheep and their tendency to go astray? Why sheep — why not cattle?

11. How does Jesus compare with an earthly shepherd and overseer? How can pastors (under-shepherds) follow Jesus' lead in their ministry?

12. What one thing have your learned so far from this study?

*Dear Jesus, our Good Shepherd, help us follow You and teach other lambs and sheep to follow you also. Amen*

NOTES:

# "The Hopeful Disciple"
### A Study of the Letters of St. Peter

## *Session #6*
## The First Letter of Peter 3:1-12

✝ ✝ ✝

**3** ¹ *Likewise, wives, be subject to your own husbands, so that even if some do not obey the word, they may be won without a word by the conduct of their wives,* ² *when they see your respectful and pure conduct.* ³ *Do not let your adorning be external – the braiding of hair and the putting on of gold jewelry, or the clothing you wear –* ⁴ *but let your adorning be the hidden person of the heart with the imperishable beauty of a gentle and quiet spirit, which in God's sight is very precious.* ⁵ *For this is how the holy women who hoped in God used to adorn themselves, by submitting to their own husbands,* ⁶ *as Sarah obeyed Abraham, calling him lord. And you are her children, if you do good and do not fear anything that is frightening.* ⁷ *Likewise, husbands, live with your wives in an understanding way, showing honor to the woman as the weaker vessel, since they are heirs with you of the grace of life, so that your prayers may not be hindered.* ⁸ *Finally, all of you, have unity of mind, sympathy, brotherly love, a tender heart, and a humble mind.* ⁹ *Do not repay evil for evil or reviling for reviling, but on the contrary, bless, for to this you were called, that you may obtain a blessing.* ¹⁰ *For,* **"Whoever desires to love life and see good days, let him keep his tongue from evil and his lips from speaking deceit;** ¹¹ **let him turn away from evil and do good; let him seek peace and pursue it.** ¹² **For**

*the eyes of the Lord are on the righteous, and his ears are open to their prayer. But the face of the Lord is against those who do evil."*

+ + +

This section takes up the duties of wives and husbands as part of the social code of the times. Peter, however, addresses it from God's perspective, not society's. Unlike similar New Testament sections (Colossians 3:18-21, Ephesians 5:22-6:4), the major focus is on the roles and duties of spouses, and nothing is said about children.

Beginning with, *"Be subject"* (verse 1), this section is intended to help bring about salvation for individuals, not invoke a subservient attitude in marriage. Subjecting one's self to another person is a voluntary act and attitude, not one to be demanded. This is done all the time among employees, in the military and in some social circles. It can therefore also be done in the family.

Voluntary subjection helps maintain peace, love and respect in relationships. Peter speaks of the wife's influence over her husband by her humble, respectful and agreeable attitude in the home. Women at that time were often quicker to follow Jesus, so Peter urges them to show the same kind of attitude to help their husband come to faith in Christ just as they have.

1. Which famous wife does Peter first mention? How are these wives *"her children?"*

Sarah was submissive Because she Become the mother of many nations As Abes wife

2. Imagine the courage of Sarah and other women of her day. What unique challenges did they have compared with women today?

3. Peter appeals to husbands to be gentle with their wives. How has the *"weaker vessel"* concept unfortunately been misused? Why might it seem an accurate description, but in fact is not?

4. What does Peter seem to be saying to men in verse 7 *("so that your prayers may not be hindered")* ?

5. Why is *"unity of mind"* important in a marital relationship? How does verse 8 show us the motives of a good relationship?

6. Verse 9 speaks of *"evil for evil and reviling for reviling."* Peter probably had been married quite a few years. How would this affect his attitude?

7. Where is the Old Testament verse located that is quoted in verse 10-12?

8. Christians live their whole lives in the presence of God. Therefore also in marriage they must display the attitudes such as Paul's "Fruit of the Spirit" in Galatians 3:22-23. What are they?

9. Why can this be so difficult in marriage?

10. How can a marriage benefit more from humility than pride?

11. How are Christian marriages helped or hindered by present day attitudes regarding marriage?

12. Today's roles of men and women in marriage favor personal rights and individualism. How does Ephesians 5:21 speak to this?

13. What can Christian single people learn from Peter in this discussion?

14. How can Christians respond when the topic of "individual rights" is brought up in conversation?

*Dear Jesus, help us love and honor one another in all our relationships. Grant that there be love, strength and cooperation in all marriages. Amen*

NOTES:

# "The Hopeful Disciple"

*A Study of the Letters of St. Peter*

## *Session #7*
## The First Letter of Peter 3:13-22

+ + +

**3** ¹³ Now who is there to harm you if you are zealous for what is good? ¹⁴ But even if you should suffer for righteousness' sake, you will be blessed. Have no fear of them, nor be troubled, ¹⁵ but in your hearts honor Christ the Lord as holy, always being prepared to make a defense to anyone who asks you for a reason for the hope that is in you; yet do it with gentleness and respect, ¹⁶ having a good conscience, so that, when you are slandered, those who revile your good behavior in Christ may be put to shame. ¹⁷ For it is better to suffer for doing good, if that should be God's will, than for doing evil. ¹⁸ For Christ also suffered once for sins, the righteous for the unrighteous, that he might bring us to God, being put to death in the flesh but made alive in the spirit, ¹⁹ in which he went and proclaimed to the spirits in prison, ²⁰ because they formerly did not obey, when God's patience waited in the days of Noah, while the ark was being prepared, in which a few, that is, eight persons, were brought safely through water. ²¹ Baptism, which corresponds to this, now saves you, not as a removal of dirt from the body but as an appeal to God for a good conscience, through the resurrection of Jesus Christ, ²² who has gone into heaven and is at the right hand of God, with angels, authorities, and powers having been subjected to him.

+ + +

In this section, we realize the difference between suffering in general and suffering for righteousness' sake (verse 14). Most often our idea of human suffering only centers around ill health, bad decisions or the evil deeds of others.

Suffering for righteousness' sake is the direct result of receiving righteousness from Jesus Christ and our living righteously through Him. Doing so always puts us on a collision course with the world's definition of how to live rightly.

The Christian must always keep in mind that our Savior has defeated God's enemies by His death on the cross. Therefore, we gain strength from His victory that will help us in any suffering and persecution.

Instead of wringing our hands over evil in the world, we ought rather to lift joyful hands in thanksgiving. The end result of suffering and persecution is not in our hands. It's in God's hands, and He will do for us what is best. When suffering and persecution come to us, then our faith is tested and strengthened.

1. In verses 13-14, Peter gives hope to believers for the times when trouble comes into their lives. Summarize that he says:


2. What does verse 15 tells us to do? Why should we be prepared?


3. Note the attitude Peter says we should have in our witness. Why is that important?

4. If a Christian is slandered, how can the attitudes of gentleness and respect effect those who witness it?

5. Why is it better to suffer for doing good? What good is any suffering?

6. In verses 18-19, Peter speaks of Christ's suffering, but it culminates in what is called the "descent into hell." This is the only passage which speaks directly of this Christian doctrine. What do you think Christ proclaimed to the people in hell?

7. Verses 20-21 mention Noah and the flood. How does Peter say this applies to baptism?

8. What is the effect of Baptism?

9. How does a *"good conscience"* come into this discussion?

10. Verse 22 almost sounds like it could be part of one of our Christian traditions. Which one?

11. Christians believe Christ is their hope when suffering comes. No real, eternal harm can come to those who believe in Christ, because no evil can take Christ from our hearts. When a Christian trusts Jesus as Lord, there is no need to fear evil, no matter what may happen to us. Christ has overcome the effects of evil.

12. Read #11 again. How can it affect our approach to all types of suffering?


13. Which do you think is worse? Losing one's family and loved ones, or losing one's faith in Jesus? Why?


14. What would you tell someone today who has lost loved ones to the evils of terrorists, drug-pushers or a tragic accident? What should you not tell them?


*Lord Jesus, You suffered for us and our loved ones. When suffering or persecution come, give us joy in knowing You will give us something far greater than what earthly life can bring or take away. Amen*

NOTES:

# "The Hopeful Disciple"

*A Study of the Letters of St. Peter*

## *Session #8*
## The First Letter of Peter 4:1-11

+ + +

**4** *¹ Since therefore Christ suffered in the flesh, arm yourselves with the same way of thinking, for whoever has suffered in the flesh has ceased from sin, ² so as to live for the rest of the time in the flesh no longer for human passions but for the will of God. ³ For the time that is past suffices for doing what the Gentiles want to do, living in sensuality, passions, drunkenness, orgies, drinking parties, and lawless idolatry. ⁴ With respect to this they are surprised when you do not join them in the same flood of debauchery, and they malign you; ⁵ but they will give account to him who is ready to judge the living and the dead. ⁶ For this is why the gospel was preached even to those who are dead, that though judged in the flesh the way people are, they might live in the spirit the way God does. ⁷ The end of all things is at hand; therefore be self-controlled and sober-minded for the sake of your prayers. ⁸ Above all, keep loving one another earnestly, since love covers a multitude of sins. ⁹ Show hospitality to one another without grumbling. ¹⁰ As each has received a gift, use it to serve one another, as good stewards of God's varied grace: ¹¹ whoever speaks, as one who speaks oracles of God; whoever serves, as one who serves by the strength that God supplies — in order that in everything God may be glorified through Jesus Christ. To him belong glory and dominion forever and ever. Amen.*

These words from God through Peter warn of what is to come. Suffering and persecution will not be easy or simple, so believers must arm themselves, not with weapons but with the *"same way of thinking"* as Peter has presented. Suffering, pain or anguish is not the worst that can happen. It can, in fact, help us to stop living in ways of the world and begin living for Christ.

Those who realize this will find they need not live only in their own power, but in Christ's power. They are not alone as they face fears or inabilities, for they have the capabilities God gives them. The ways of Jesus Christ give life now and life eternally. Those who try to find peace and joy only by worldly ways will find emptiness.

1. What do you think Peter means that suffering helps us *"cease from sin"* (verse 2)? How is this moving "against the grain" of life?

2. What do you think *"passions of the flesh"* (verse 2) means?

3. Verse 3 lists some of the things the Gentiles do. Sound familiar? How can Christians see a parallel between themselves and Jews?

4. Verse 5 says they will give account to *"him who is ready to judge the living and the dead."* Everyone will face judgment by Christ (Matthew 25:31-446). So how should we be concerned?

5. In verse 6, *"those who are dead"* is not preaching to dead people, but to those who died before the return of Christ. What main "ingredient" is necessary for people to live eternally? How could they have it?

6. What do you think *"live in the spirit the way God does"* means?

7. What is meant by *"love covers a multitude of sins"* in verse 8? What kind of love is that? How is this done?

8. Verse 9 may mean some believers struggle with hospitality. How can people *"show hospitality"* today? How might doing that become a burden?

9. In verse 10, Peter sounds very much like Paul, encouraging the people to use the gifts God has given them. How does Peter want them to use their gifts? What can this teach us today?

10. What does Peter call Christians in verse 10?

11. Peter mentions only two gifts, speaking and serving and that they can use these gifts to help God's people. Have you ever taken a test to discover your spiritual gifts? If so, what are they?

12. The words, "*in order that in everything God may be glorified through Jesus Christ*" give purpose to our acts of service and hospitality. What's your favorite way of showing hospitality?

13. The last part of verse 11 is a kind of doxology: *"To him belong glory and dominion forever and ever. Amen."* What is a "doxology"?

14. What part of this section gives you hope? Why?

*Lord Jesus, keep us in Your grace so that we may not fall to the temptations of this world. Amen*

NOTES:

# "The Hopeful Disciple"

*A Study of the Letters of St. Peter*

## *Session #9*
## The First Letter of Peter 4:12-19

+ + +

**4** [12] *Beloved, do not be surprised at the fiery trial when it comes upon you to test you, as though something strange were happening to you.* [13] *But rejoice insofar as you share Christ's sufferings, that you may also rejoice and be glad when his glory is revealed.* [14] *If you are insulted for the name of Christ, you are blessed, because the Spirit of glory and of God rests upon you.* [15] *But let none of you suffer as a murderer or a thief or an evildoer or as a meddler.* [16] *Yet if anyone suffers as a Christian, let him not be ashamed, but let him glorify God in that name.* [17] *For it is time for judgment to begin at the household of God; and if it begins with us, what will be the outcome for those who do not obey the gospel of God?* [18] *And,* **"If the righteous is scarcely saved, what will become of the ungodly and the sinner?"** [19] *Therefore let those who suffer according to God's will entrust their souls to a faithful Creator while doing good.*

+ + +

Peter's tone becomes more serious. Facing "fiery trials" are words no one wishes to hear. There would have been stories circulating about the persecutions that were taking place, stories that affected Gentiles more than Jews. Believers were to show love, and this would

33

leave them vulnerable for unbelievers to take advantage of their hospitality or gentle behavior.

Suffering is what Christians will face because Christ their Lord has already faced it. In Matthew 10:24 Jesus said, *"A disciple is not above his teacher,"* so Peter now tells believers they can expect unbelievers to resist their way of life harshly.

Their Lord was killed for His message, and both Peter and Paul had already been imprisoned for their faith. Followers of Jesus of Nazareth must realize the very definite possibility they, too, would be imprisoned, persecuted and even killed for their faith. Being a follower of Jesus would not be easy!

Christians have suffered for Christ throughout the ages. Perhaps the greatest earthly enemies of Christ have been followers of Islam. Few American Christians today can accurately know what it means to suffer for their faith the way that European Christians did during WWII or African and Arabic Christians are suffering today at the hands of Muslim terrorists.

The important message Peter would have us know today is that suffering will come to Christians. We need to realize this and expect it so we do not reject our faith just because we are persecuted

1. Verse 12 speaks of *"fiery trials"* which will come to test them. It may seem strange that God would allow His people to suffer. How are Christians suffering today?

2. Verse 13 states we should rejoice in this suffering, because we share in what Christ has experienced. When can we expect to *"be glad"* in this suffering?

3. What might the world think when they see Christians suffer? Why should we not expect them to help Christians?


4. What recent examples come to mind of Christians suffering for their faith? Why do people think America should come to their aid? Why might America not do so?


5. What is the main point of verse 14? Why will it not be easy?


6. There is also suffering for wrongdoing (theft, murder, meddling). Why does Peter urge them not to be caught in these?


7. Verse 16 says we need not be ashamed of persecution for following Christ's commands. How can a person *"glorify God"* in persecution? Could you?


8. Have you ever felt you were being spiritually lazy or uninvolved because you are not being persecuted? What do you think Peter might say if you admitted that?


9. Verse 17 presents a chilling warning: *"It is time for judgment to begin at the household of God."* What would you think if you heard a sermon on that topic? What would you tell the preacher?

10. What is inferred by verse 17 about those who do not receive the Gospel? What do you think Peter would say will happen to them?


11. Where is the Old Testament passage quoted in verse 18? What will become of the ungodly person?



12. What is meant by *"entrusting their souls to a faithful Creator"* in verse 19? How can we do that today?


*Lord Jesus, give us a strong, enduring faith when we come in contact with trials and suffering. Amen*

NOTES:

# "The Hopeful Disciple"
## A Study of the Letters of St. Peter

### *Session #10*
### The First Letter of Peter 5:1-14

+ + +

**5** ¹ *So I exhort the elders among you, as a fellow elder and a witness of the sufferings of Christ, as well as a partaker in the glory that is going to be revealed:* ² *shepherd the flock of God that is among you, exercising oversight, not under compulsion, but willingly, as God would have you; not for shameful gain, but eagerly;* ³ *not domineering over those in your charge, but being examples to the flock.* ⁴ *And when the chief Shepherd appears, you will receive the unfading crown of glory.* ⁵ *Likewise, you who are younger, be subject to the elders. Clothe yourselves, all of you, with humility toward one another, for* **"God opposes the proud but gives grace to the humble."** ⁶ *Humble yourselves, therefore, under the mighty hand of God so that at the proper time he may exalt you,* ⁷ *casting all your anxieties on him, because he cares for you.* ⁸ *Be sober-minded; be watchful. Your adversary the devil prowls around like a roaring lion, seeking someone to devour.* ⁹ *Resist him, firm in your faith, knowing that the same kinds of suffering are being experienced by your brotherhood throughout the world.* ¹⁰ *And after you have suffered a little while, the God of all grace, who has called you to his eternal glory in Christ, will himself restore, confirm, strengthen, and establish you.* ¹¹ *To him be the dominion forever and ever. Amen.* ¹² *By Silvanus, a faithful brother as I regard him, I have* *written briefly to you, exhorting and declaring that this is the true grace of God. Stand firm in it. [13] She who is at Babylon, who is likewise chosen, sends you greetings, and so does Mark, my son. [14] Greet one another with the kiss of love. Peace to all of you who are in Christ.*

✝   ✝   ✝

Following a pattern he may have learned from Paul's letters, Peter speaks in his closing comments to the pastoral leaders (elders) in the churches of Asia Minor. He believes the End Times are near, so he encourages them to care for the flock God has given each of them. These good words for pastors are often today read at their ordination or installation at a congregation.

Peter encourages younger leaders to pay humble attention to their elders. Humble service will keep the different parts of the Body of Christ together and will keep Satan from dividing the Body, which he constantly seeks to do.

Peter compares pastoral service to suffering for the sake of Christ. Being a pastor will not be an easy task, but those who are called by God will be restored and strengthened. He concludes with greetings to Silvanus and Mark.

---

1. Peter greets the pastors as a fellow pastor. He has witnessed both sufferings and glory. Can you recall a time or two when Peter saw Jesus in His glory?

38

2. Why does Peter tell the pastors to be willing in their service? What might make them feel compelled to do their work (verse 2)?


3. Verse 3 speaks of leadership. What are the best qualities you like to see in a pastor?


4. What do you think is the *"unfading crown of glory"* (verse 4)?


5. Which Old Testament verse is quoted in verse 5?


6. Humility is a good leadership quality. How can Satan use pride and self-exaltation as weapons against God's people?


7. Verse 7 is a very comforting passage. Although it is part of a longer sentence, most of us consider these words as one verse: *"Cast all your cares on Him, because He cares for you."* How does that verse speak to you?


8. Verse 8 describes Satan as a prowling, roaring man-eater. He tempts people by either making us fear him or making us forget or deny him. Which do you see Satan doing today?


9. What have you found is the best way to resist Satan?

10. In verse 10 Peter says God will rescue them to His eternal glory. Along the way, He will *"restore, confirm, strengthen and establish you."* What is meant by "establish"?


11. After another brief doxology, Peter sends greetings. Silvanus is often another name for Silas, a partner Paul had during his journeys. Whom do you think is the man named Mark?


12. *"She who is in Babylon"* – who might this be?


13. The "kiss of love" was an actual kiss, usually on both cheeks. Do you know of any Middle Eastern countries where this is done?


14. Did any part of this final passage give you hope?


*Dear Lord, protect us from all evil and keep us in Your care. Amen*

NOTES:

# "The Hopeful Disciple"

*A Study of the Letters of St. Peter*

## Session #11

+ + +

### Overview of 2 Peter

**AUTHOR**

The author is Simon Peter, an eyewitness of the transfiguration and the resurrection. He states this is his second letter to Christians in 3:1. Though a few Biblical scholars have tried to disprove this, the early church accepted Peter as author.

**THEME**

While 1 Peter speaks of God's grace in the trials of persecution, 2 Peter speaks of God's grace amid the trials of false teachers. Both letters encourage the reader towards hope in the Lord in the face of all kinds of trials.

2 Peter is often called the "Epistle of Knowledge." It gives true knowledge in Christ in order (1) to strengthen the Christian's hope, (2) to defend Christian hope against the attacks of error (false teaching) and heresy (maintaining false teaching as the truth), and (3) to protect hope against doubt.

While 1 Peter was written to keep hope alive and strong in people under duress, 2 Peter was written to maintain hope that is pure and strong in people whose hope may be threatened by false teaching or weakened by doubt.

## LUTHER ON 2 PETER

*"This epistle is written against those who think that Christian faith can be without works. Therefore he exhorts them to test themselves by good works and become sure of their faith, just as one knows a tree by its fruit."* (Luther's Works, Vol. 5, p. 391)

## DATE

2 Peter was written near the end of Peter's life and after he had written the prior letter to which he refers in 3:1. Peter was martyred during the reign of Nero, between 65 and 68 AD. (Do you remember what "BC" and "AD" stand for?)

## RECIPIENTS

Peter writes to mature believers (1:1) *"who have obtained a faith of equal standing with ours."*

+ + +

# The Second Letter of Peter 1:1-12
+ + +

**1** ¹ *Simeon Peter, a servant and apostle of Jesus Christ, To those who have obtained a faith of equal standing with ours by the righteousness of our God and Savior Jesus Christ: ² May grace and peace be multiplied to you in the knowledge of God and of Jesus our Lord. ³ His divine power has granted to us all things that pertain to life and godliness, through the knowledge of him who called us to his own glory and excellence, ⁴ by which he has granted to us his precious and very great promises, so that through them you may become partakers of the divine nature, having escaped from the*

*corruption that is in the world because of sinful desire.*
*⁵ For this very reason, make every effort to supplement
your faith with virtue, and virtue with knowledge, ⁶ and
knowledge with self-control, and self-control with
steadfastness, and steadfastness with godliness, ⁷ and
godliness with brotherly affection, and brotherly
affection with love. ⁸ For if these qualities are yours and
are increasing, they keep you from being ineffective or
unfruitful in the knowledge of our Lord Jesus Christ.
⁹ For whoever lacks these qualities is so nearsighted that
he is blind, having forgotten that he was cleansed from
his former sins. ¹⁰ Therefore, brothers, be all the more
diligent to confirm your calling and election, for if you
practice these qualities you will never fall. ¹¹ For in this
way there will be richly provided for you an entrance
into the eternal kingdom of our Lord and Savior Jesus
Christ. ¹² Therefore I intend always to remind you of
these qualities, though you know them and are
established in the truth that you have.*

+ + +

1. Verse 1, "Simeon" and "Simon" are the same name. The
reference to *"equal standing"* denotes time has passed since his
last letter and maturing of faith. Note in these sessions how his
message is different from 1 Peter.

2. Verse 2 is Peter's salutation and blessing. Note the considerate
and kind manner of letter writing of that day.

3. Verse 3 — *"all things that pertain to life and godliness"* are
those gifts God grants to believers. How has God blessed your life
with His gifts?

4. Verse 4 — *"so that through them you may become partakers of the divine nature..."* What does this tell us of God's purpose in giving us His gifts?




5. In verses 5-7, Peter lists the outcome of Christian attitudes:
With faith comes _____, then _____
then_____, then_____, then
_____, then_____, and finally,_____.

6. What do you think Peter means by being *"ineffective or unfruitful"* in verse 8? With regards to what is he writing this?


7. In verse 9, Peter says in strong language the qualities necessary for believers to have. What do you think he would he say if a believer didn't have such qualities?


8. Where has Peter spoken of *"calling and election"* before?


9. How does *"entrance into the eternal kingdom"* come in verse 11? How does God's grace factor into our reception of eternal life?


*Thank You, Lord for Your grace and mercy. Amen*

NOTES:

# "The Hopeful Disciple"
### *A Study of the Letters of St. Peter*

## *Session #12*
## The Second Letter of Peter 1:13-21
### + + +

**1** <sup></sup> *13 I think it right, as long as I am in this body, to stir you up by way of reminder, 14 since I know that the putting off of my body will be soon, as our Lord Jesus Christ made clear to me. 15 And I will make every effort so that after my departure you may be able at any time to recall these things. 16 For we did not follow cleverly devised myths when we made known to you the power and coming of our Lord Jesus Christ, but we were eyewitnesses of his majesty. 17 For when he received honor and glory from God the Father, and the voice was borne to him by the Majestic Glory,* **"This is my beloved Son, with whom I am well pleased,"** *18 we ourselves heard this very voice borne from heaven, for we were with him on the holy mountain. 19 And we have the prophetic word more fully confirmed, to which you will do well to pay attention as to a lamp shining in a dark place, until the day dawns and the morning star rises in your hearts, 20 knowing this first of all, that no prophecy of Scripture comes from someone's own interpretation. 21 For no prophecy was ever produced by the will of man, but men spoke from God as they were carried along by the Holy Spirit.*

### + + +

1. To what do you think *"putting off of my body"* refers?

2. How does verse 15 show Peter's purpose in writing this letter?

3. Peter's reference in verse 16 to *"cleverly devised myths"* shows that already in the early church there were false teachings being spread around. One of the purposes of his writing was to urge people to resist false teachers and remain true to the Gospel. What kinds of false teachers do we see today?

4. *"What we received glory and honor from God the Father"* refers to what event? How does this reference identify the author?

5. Where is the source the passage quoted in verse 17?

6. The exact location of the *"Holy Mountain"* (Transfiguration) of verse 18 is unknown, but tradition has assigned it to Mount Tabor, a noticeable peak in central Israel near the south outlet of the Sea of Galilee. Can you find Mount Tabor on a map?

7. How might locating biblical places help our faith?

8. Peter states he heard the *"very voice from heaven,"* another reference to his authorship. Why do you think might some scholars wish to prove Peter was not the author?

9. In verse 19, what might *"the prophetic word"* be referring to?

10. *"Lamp shining in a dark place"* is another biblical metaphor of the difference between "light" and "darkness." How do these passages speak of that difference?

Psalm 119:105_____

Genesis 1:4_____

Psalm 27:1_____

Matthew 6:23_____

John 8:12_____

Revelation 21:23_____

11. *"No prophecy of Scripture comes from someone's own interpretation"* (verse 21) might be news to those who continually seek to find a date for the end of the world. In Matthew 24:36, who didn't even know when that day would be? Who does know?

12. 2 Peter 1:21 *("For no prophecy was ever produced by the will of man, but men spoke from God as they were carried along by the Holy Spirit.")* is so important it deserves extensive examination. It is the basis for the Christian doctrine of inspiration. Let's look at it carefully:

13. *"No prophecy was ever produced by the will of man,.."* This speaks of prophesy from God, the true God of Holy Scripture, and the words He wishes to have recorded. How do some other religions rely on prophecy of the future?


14. *"Men spoke from God..."* The words of the Bible are given us from the Holy Spirit. God speaks in His Word. How do we know?


15. *"As they were carried along by the Holy Spirit."* The source of God's prophesy is the Holy Spirit. One of the tasks of the Holy Spirit is to convince people of all ages that Jesus is the true Son of God, the Savior of the world. Because the Holy Spirit wants to be believe in Jesus, He directed people to write *"God's words"* about *"God's Word."* How are the two phrases different?


16. The King James Version translates this verse: *"Holy men of God spoke as they were moved by the Holy Ghost."* It is as clear a translation as has been given in English. What translation did you have when you memorized verses?


*Thank You, Lord, for giving us Your Holy Word. Amen*

NOTES:

# "The Hopeful Disciple"

*A Study of the Letters of St. Peter*

## *Session #13*
## The Second Letter of Peter 2:1-10a

+ + +

**2** ¹ *But false prophets also arose among the people, just as there will be false teachers among you, who will secretly bring in destructive heresies, even denying the Master who bought them, bringing upon themselves swift destruction.* ² *And many will follow their sensuality, and because of them the way of truth will be blasphemed.* ³ *And in their greed they will exploit you with false words. Their condemnation from long ago is not idle, and their destruction is not asleep.* ⁴ *For if God did not spare angels when they sinned, but cast them into hell and committed them to chains of gloomy darkness to be kept until the judgment;* ⁵ *if he did not spare the ancient world, but preserved Noah, a herald of righteousness, with seven others, when he brought a flood upon the world of the ungodly;* ⁶ *if by turning the cities of Sodom and Gomorrah to ashes he condemned them to extinction, making them an example of what is going to happen to the ungodly;* ⁷ *and if he rescued righteous Lot, greatly distressed by the sensual conduct of the wicked* ⁸ *(for as that righteous man lived among them day after day, he was tormenting his righteous soul over their lawless deeds that he saw and heard);* ⁹ *then the Lord knows how to rescue the godly from trials, and to keep the unrighteous under punishment until the day of judgment,* ¹⁰ *and especially those who* *indulge in the lust of defiling passion and despise authority.*

+ + +

There has always been some measure of false teaching in the Christian Church, due mostly to the teachers or students who fall short in their understanding of the teachings of Jesus Christ. False teachings (error) are less a problem then the false teachers who maintain their false teachings are the truth (heresy), and insist that others follow them. Peter warns against them in this section.

Numerous New Testament passages warn against accepting false teachings. Some false teachers were believers, but some were not, and they led the people astray for selfish motives and purposes.

1. Peter is saying just as false teachers have arisen elsewhere, so also they can expect false teachers among them as well. Which words in verse 1 make you wonder if false teachers were believers?

2. To what kind of destruction is Peter referring?

3. What do you think is meant by *"way of sensuality"* in verse 2?

4. What is meant by *"the way of truth is blasphemed"*?

5. What kind of personal gain would move some people to become false teachers?


6. Peter refers to three biblical events in verses 4-8. Which are they?

a._____

b. _____

c. _____


7. Of what does fate of those angels in verse 4 remind us?


8. What are the *"chains of gloomy darkness"*?


9. How was Noah a *"herald of righteousness"* in verse 5?


10. In verses 6-7 Peter refers to the destruction of Sodom and Gomorrah for their sins. Modern critics say the sins of those cities were not sexual immorality, but the people's lack of being kind and welcoming towards strangers. If that's so, isn't their punishment harsh? Why would critics deny the biblical record of their sins?

11. Abram's nephew Lot is often criticized as being weak for choosing the better land of around Sodom. But how does verse 8 characterize Lot?


12. See Genesis 19:1. Where is Lot sitting when the angels arrived? What does this tell us about Lot's character? Who were those chosen to "sit in the gate" in the ancient cities?


13. What is Peter's point in verse 8 about these past events?


14. Verse 10 warns us against the _____ of defiling _____ and _____ _____. The first warning there is understandable. Why would Peter warn against despising authority?


15. How does this section help us understand a little more about Christian hope?


*Help us, Lord, to follow Your Word and not stray from its message of eternal life in Jesus. Amen*

NOTES:

# "The Hopeful Disciple"
### A Study of the Letters of St. Peter

## *Session #14*
## The Second Letter of Peter 2:10b-22
### + + +

**2** *¹⁰ Bold and willful, they do not tremble as they blaspheme the glorious ones, ¹¹ whereas angels, though greater in might and power, do not pronounce a blasphemous judgment against them before the Lord. ¹² But these, like irrational animals, creatures of instinct, born to be caught and destroyed, blaspheming about matters of which they are ignorant, will also be destroyed in their destruction, ¹³ suffering wrong as the wage for their wrongdoing. They count it pleasure to revel in the daytime. They are blots and blemishes, reveling in their deceptions, while they feast with you. ¹⁴ They have eyes full of adultery, insatiable for sin. They entice unsteady souls. They have hearts trained in greed. Accursed children! ¹⁵ Forsaking the right way, they have gone astray. They have followed the way of Balaam, the son of Beor, who loved gain from wrongdoing, ¹⁶ but was rebuked for his own transgression; a speechless donkey spoke with human voice and restrained the prophet's madness. ¹⁷ These are waterless springs and mists driven by a storm. For them the gloom of utter darkness has been reserved. ¹⁸ For, speaking loud boasts of folly, they entice by sensual passions of the flesh those who are barely escaping from those who live in error. ¹⁹ They promise them freedom, but they themselves are slaves of corruption. For whatever overcomes a person, to that he*

53

*is enslaved.* <sup>20</sup> *For if, after they have escaped the defilements of the world through the knowledge of our Lord and Savior Jesus Christ, they are again entangled in them and overcome, the last state has become worse for them than the first.* <sup>21</sup> *For it would have been better for them never to have known the way of righteousness than after knowing it to turn back from the holy commandment delivered to them.* <sup>22</sup> *What the true proverb says has happened to them:* **"The dog returns to its own vomit, and the sow, after washing herself, returns to wallow in the mire."**

+ + +

1. Peter continues his warning against false teachers. What does he call them in verse 10?


2. Peter says false teachers are even more bold than the angels who would never _____ against God. Why do you think would angels be so fearful of doing this?


3. In verse 12, he adds more adjectives of false teachers. They are _____, and creatures of _____, blaspheming about matters of which they are _____. What will eventually happen to them?


4. In Verse 13a, Peter seems to be condemning them to hell. Why is Peter so harsh?

54

5. Verse 13b says false teachers even revel in the daytime. Sinne. usually revel at night, but these bold ones have no shame. Peter calls them _____ and _____. As he showed during his discipleship, Peter does not mince words!

6. In verse 14, Peter condemns false teachers as harshly as he would condemn the worst of sinners. He even says they are _____ _____. Why do you think Peter is being so hard on them?

7. Who was Balaam in verse 15 (see Numbers 22:14-6)? What unique event happened to Balaam? (Numbers 22:27-28)?

8. Peter isn't done with his condemnation of false prophets. In verse 17, what does he call them? Why would these terms show his contempt of them?

9. What does the *"gloom of utter darkness"* signify?

10. In verses 18-19, Peter says false prophets promise their followers a better life. But what will they actually become?

11. Read verse 20 and compare it to Matthew 23:15. Why do you think Peter may have often recalled these words of Jesus?

e 21 has a chilling message. What does Peter seem to be
ᵧ there?

13. Where in the Old Testament is the passage Peter quotes in
verse 22? Why do you think he quotes it?

14. In Matthew 23, Jesus condemns the Pharisees for leading
people astray. Peter is echoing the words of his Teacher and Lord
Jesus. What Jesus say of them in Luke 17:2?

15. Even though this passage is all Law and no Gospel, why could
it still give Peter's listeners hope in their daily lives?

NOTES:

# "The Hopeful Disciple"
*A Study of the Letters of St. Peter*

## *Session #15*
## The Second Letter of Peter 3:1-10
+ + +

**3** *¹ This is now the second letter that I am writing to you, beloved. In both of them I am stirring up your sincere mind by way of reminder, ² that you should remember the predictions of the holy prophets and the commandment of the Lord and Savior through your apostles, ³ knowing this first of all, that scoffers will come in the last days with scoffing, following their own sinful desires. ⁴ They will say,* **"Where is the promise of his coming? For ever since the fathers fell asleep, all things are continuing as they were from the beginning of creation."** *⁵ For they deliberately overlook this fact, that the heavens existed long ago, and the earth was formed out of water and through water by the word of God, ⁶ and that by means of these the world that then existed was deluged with water and perished. ⁷ But by the same word the heavens and earth that now exist are stored up for fire, being kept until the day of judgment and destruction of the ungodly. ⁸ But do not overlook this one fact, beloved, that with the Lord one day is as a thousand years, and a thousand years as one day. ⁹ The Lord is not slow to fulfill his promise as some count slowness, but is patient toward you, not wishing that any should perish, but that all should reach repentance. ¹⁰ But the day of the Lord will come like a thief, and then the heavens will pass away with a roar, and the heavenly bodies will be burned up and* *dissolved, and the earth and the works that are done on it will be exposed.*

+   +   +

Like Paul, Peter is zealous to guard those under his care from error and false teachings. He knows the people will be eager to learn and thus may be tempted to follow teachers who will lead them astray. Whereas Paul used refined words and examples to lead and guide the people, Peter approached the problem head-on, holding nothing back and warning them in severe words. We would expect nothing less from this man.

This section shows Peter's willingness to *"tell it like it is"* in his warnings. Christians want to hear fact, not fancy, and are endeared to Peter by his feelings such as we see in these verses.

1. What basic information does 3:1 give us about the author of this letter? Why should it matter who the author is?

2. In verse 2, Peter says he wants his readers to remember the _____ of the Old Testament _____, as well as the _____ of the _____ through the _____. Why is it important to look to the "primary sources" for the basis of one's faith?

3. In verse 3, what is a "scoffer"?

4. Where in the Old Testament is the passage quoted in verse 4?

5. Verse 5 almost sounds like Peter is talking about modern skeptics. Which words denote the method God used in creation?

6. Scientists tells us water is one of the most important elements for a planet to sustain life. How much of the earth's surface is covered by water? How much of our bodies are made of water?

7. How important is water in the Christian faith? Of what can water also become a source in verse 6?

8. How does verse 7 hint that the destruction of the earth will come about?

9. Verse 8 contains a well-known fact, that time is not the same with God as it is with human beings. What do you think life would be like if we were not bound by either time or space?

10. Verse 9 should give us great hope. What does it say?

11. Why do you think is God so patient with sinful people? How does Paul agree with Peter in 1 Timothy 2:3-4?

12. In verse 10a, Peter echoes the words of Paul. What does Paul tell us in 1 Thessalonians 5:2?



13. It's helpful to know that the Apostles were aware of some of the writings being sent around from church to church. Peter would have read some of Paul's writings, and Paul would have read the letters of Peter. Why would this be important?



14. In verse 10b, how does Peter describe the end of the world and the prelude to Judgment Day?



15. How does the message of verse 10 give Christians hope?


*Help us be ready for Your coming, Lord Jesus. Amen*

NOTES:

# "The Hopeful Disciple"
## A Study of the Letters of St. Peter

### *Session #16*
## The Second Letter of Peter 3:11-18
+ + +

**3** *¹¹ Since all these things are thus to be dissolved, what sort of people ought you to be in lives of holiness and godliness, ¹² waiting for and hastening the coming of the day of God, because of which the heavens will be set on fire and dissolved, and the heavenly bodies will melt as they burn! ¹³ But according to his promise we are waiting for new heavens and a new earth in which righteousness dwells. ¹⁴ Therefore, beloved, since you are waiting for these, be diligent to be found by him without spot or blemish, and at peace. ¹⁵ And count the patience of our Lord as salvation, just as our beloved brother Paul also wrote to you according to the wisdom given him, ¹⁶ as he does in all his letters when he speaks in them of these matters. There are some things in them that are hard to understand, which the ignorant and unstable twist to their own destruction, as they do the other Scriptures. ¹⁷ You therefore, beloved, knowing this beforehand, take care that you are not carried away with the error of lawless people and lose your own stability. ¹⁸ But grow in the grace and knowledge of our Lord and Savior Jesus Christ. To him be the glory both now and to the day of eternity. Amen.*

+ + +

In this final section, Peter answers the question Christians often ask themselves, *"How then shall we live?"* Knowing what we do about the grace of God in Jesus Christ, what sort of lives should we live as we await His Second Coming?

Scientists who rely on human reason will quote their tables of ages and times, citing how the world came to be and how it will end. The believer in Christ wants to know the best way to spend the remaining days that God gives us. They also know by faith that God will end in His own good time what He began. And it will probably be far sooner than secular scientists believe.

1. Verse 11 tells us all will be "dissolved" in Judgment Day. Such words should make us consider how we should live as we wait. What two words here does Peter use in summing up our lives?

2. Verse 12a speaks of *"waiting for and hastening"* the day. Do you think he means godly and holy lives of Christians will make the end of the world come sooner? If not, what do the words mean?

3. Considering the language of verse 12b, what sort of conditions would bring about an end of the world that would contain fire, melting and burning? Have you heard of any such kinds of scientific possibilities where this might happen?

4. Peter speaks in verse 13 of the coming *"new heavens and new earth."* Are there other places in the Bible that speak of this new era? Can you find one?


5. What kind of "righteousness" would dwell in this *"new heavens and new earth"* that God would give us?



6. When will He give it?


7. In verse 14, Peter tells the people how they should live until Christ comes again, *"Be diligent to be found by him without spot or blemish, and at peace."* Why is there so little peace in our world today? Is the same true in the Christian church?



8. In verse 15, Peter shows his warm attitude towards Paul. He says, *"according to the wisdom given him."* Peter and Paul both know their wisdom is a gift from God, not of human intellect. What do humanists today believe is the source of human intellect?



9. In verse 16, what words show the people have also read other writings? What words show Paul's teachings may have been more difficult to understand?



10. What does verse 17 tell us of Peter's concern for them?

11. Which words show that Peter wants them to grow in their faith in Jesus?




12. The final sentence is Peter's "doxology," a term that comes from two Greek words that together mean *"word of praise."* What do we usually think of when we hear the word "doxology"?




13. The First and Second letters of Peter are a wonderful gift from God. Write one blessing you have received from this study:

_____

_____


14. In what way have these letters increased your hope in Jesus Christ?


*Lord Jesus Christ, we thank You for the Apostle Peter who served You and Your Church with his faith and example. Help us to follow his words that come to us from Your Holy Spirit. Amen*

*Robert L. Tasler*

Rev. Robert L. Tasler is a native of Windom, Minnesota, and a career pastor in the Lutheran Church-Missouri Synod, a conservative Lutheran body in fellowship with dozens of similar churches around the world. A 1971 ordained graduate of Concordia Seminary, St. Louis, Missouri, Bob has served parishes in North Dakota, California, Utah and Colorado.

He and his wife Carol are retired and divide their time between Colorado and Arizona. They are parents of Brian, a Denver business executive in a non-profit organization, and Chuck and his wife Debbie, Christian Day School Teachers in Phoenix, as well as proud grandparents of three.

Author's other works are listed in the front of this book and can be found in detail at: http://www.bobtasler.com.

Made in the USA
San Bernardino, CA
22 November 2014